THE CAT-PHABET

BY
ARIANA KLEPAC
& PETE SMITH

A GUIDE TO OUR FURRY OVERLORDS — FROM A TO Z

**Smith
Street
Books**

In association with Ariana Klepac Publishing

INTRODUCTION

This book has been designed as a helpful 'user's manual' for humans. If you already own a cat and want to know more about them, or if you are about to step into the world of fur for the first time, *The Cat-phabet* gives you an insight into what you can expect. On the one hand, you can look forward to plenty of loving warm snuggles, head bumps and purring. However, on the other hand, you'd better buckle up for those dawn wakeup calls, feedtime reminders on the minute every minute, and never being allowed to go to the bathroom on your own ever again.

The other thing you'll have to get used to is that your cat will be in charge, not you. You might think you're the boss, as you weigh ten times more and the cat is your pet and therefore under your control. But you'd be wrong.

OK, at first it does seem as if you call the shots as you show Kitty around, make him feel at home by buying him personalised food bowls and Sylvester-themed cat beds stuffed with duck down, and feel proud – and a little smug – that this little creature looks up to you, follows you around and relies on you for everything. But gradually, imperceptibly, as you fall further and further under Kitty's spell, the situation flips.

Six weeks ago you lazed around in your luxury king-sized bed, but now Kitty owns seven-eighths of it and you happily, although somewhat precariously, sleep on a narrow strip at the very edge. Your smartphone used to be perfectly adequate for your needs, but you've had to upgrade to the most expensive model with ample room for the 650 high-definition snaps of Kitty you take each day. You used to love going out and partying late but now, when a friend calls with an invitation, with the RSVP on your lips, one look at those adorable green eyes and you decide you would rather stay in and watch the *Aristocats* movie with Kitty – again.

But there's one thing you can be sure of – it's all absolutely worth it.

is for . . .

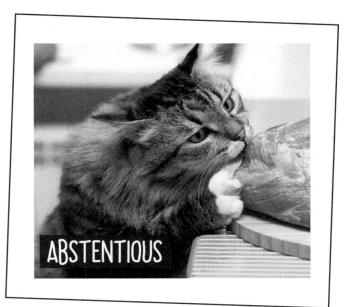

Abstentious Cats are waistline-conscious and will only ever eat just the right amount to satsify their appetite. They are more than happy to go without if their 'love handles' start to become too noticeable.

Academic Everyone appreciates a good book and cats are no different. They are more than willing to tackle the great tomes of the past literary masters – as these provide greater comfort as makeshift beds and hideouts.

A CAPELLA

A capella In the evening, one can often hear the strains of the local cat A Cappella Society beginning their weekly rehearsal in the street. How community spirited of them to provide their beautiful music for free.

ACCEPTING

Accepting Cats understand and respect the word 'no'. There's no comeback. No questions asked.

Accomplished Cats are high achievers. Their skills know no bounds.

ACCOMPLISHED

ACTIVE

Active Cats are built for speed. They can sprint up to 30 miles per hour. It is magical to witness their muscles rippling as they bound down the street, cheetah-like, in hot pursuit of that annoying Tabby at Number 20.

ACUPUNCTURIST

Acupuncturist The art of acupuncture was originally inspired by the pleasant sensation of being clawed by a cat. Cats are natural masters of this soothing and healing art.

AESTHETE

AFFECTIONATE

AFFORDABLE

Aesthete No one appreciates an object of beauty more than a cat. Sometimes the effect can be so overwhelming that the cat is forced to push the object to the floor.

Affectionate There's nothing a cat loves so much as to be ruthlessly hugged and squeezed by his owner. Just one look at his happy little face and you can tell he is begging for more.

Affordable Cats cost almost nothing to keep. They are happy with whatever generic cat food is on hand and never fuss.

AGENT PROVOCATEUR

AGILE

AGORAPHOBIC

Agent provocateur
If the dog chooses to take the bait and attempt the suggested dare to jump onto and pirouette on the small side table, it's his fault. He must bear the consequences alone. Not the cat's fault.

Agile Unlike the cat's furred mammalian cousins, such as the manic dog and the blundering bear, the cat is a master of non-slip dexterity.

Agoraphobic Cats don't like going outdoors. Even when the door is left wide open for hours at a time, you can be sure they will choose to remain indoors and never make a bolt for freedom or for the kebab shop on the corner.

AIRBORNE

ALLERGIC

Airborne It's a little known fact that cats can fly, but the conditions have to be just right. The sound of a spoon being tapped on a tin of cat food will create the necessary 'lift force' to enable the cat to take flight in order to reach the food before an impatient human removes the bowl with indecent haste.

Allergic Human cat-lovers are lucky that cats give them the time of day, let alone cuddle up to them – considering their terrible allergies to human hair and saliva.

Ambitious Cats have a sense that they are more powerful than their small stature suggests. They can eat three times their bodyweight in food and have no qualms in facing off with dogs over twice their size.

Amicable Cats have got a bad reputation for being standoffish, but they are approachable and ready for snuggles at all times.

Avant garde Always leaders and never followers, the work that cats have done in the field of avant garde art has to be seen to be believed.

AMBITIOUS

AVANT GARDE

AMICABLE

B is for . . .

BILINGUAL

Bilingual When cats have their noses pressed up against the cages of small furry animals, such as hamsters, they are simply enjoying a chat in order to practise their Hamsterese.

Black belt You may have noticed that many dogs are wary of cats and give them a wide berth. That's because they are painfully aware that most cats have a black belt in fur-jitsu.

Blue steel The 'blue steel' look was first created by a startled orange and white Tabby by the name of Brian. His expression was induced by the sight of his owner bringing home a Scottish Fold to be his 'new best friend'.

HI-YA!

BLACK BELT

BLUE STEEL

Board game champion

When the board games come out at holiday time, the family cat is the first one to the table. He likes to sit inside the lid to obscure the instructions – this way he is assured of an easy win.

Bohemian Cats have long been associated with the bohemian lifestyle. There's a gypsy vagabond spirit lurking in every cat.

Brainy Cats' high level of intelligence means they will never be fooled into thinking the rustling of a generic plastic bag by their human owner (in order to coax them off the bed) is in fact a packet of their favourite chicken chews.

ooh la la

BOHEMIAN

$$E = mc^2$$

BRAINY

BREAKDANCER

BURLESQUE

Brave Rottweilers, monster trucks and Harley Davidson motorbikes are no sweat for the average cat. However, the phrase 'flea bath' is another matter altogether.

Breakdancer You might think Kitty is just having a creative scratch, but in fact he's practising his paw glide moves.

Burlesque Shameless show-offs all of them, cats enjoy putting on an impromptu burlesque perfomance. It's a great way for cats to let off steam, especially at those 'special' times of the year.

is for...

CABINET MAKER

CABLE GUY

CAFFEINATED

Cabinet maker When assembling flat-pack furniture, your cat will be a constant presence. He likes to ensure that no screws have been left in the box.

Cable guy Don't admonish your cat when she's tangled in cables. She knows what she's doing and has a Catificate to prove it.

Caffeinated Just like humans, cats require coffee to get going. Never leave your cup unattended.

CALCULATING

CALORIE COUNTING

CAMERA SHY

20

Calculating Cats are not stupid – they know how many treats come in that green packet.

Calorie counting Cats will always prefer the healthy option. They will reach for fruit or vegetables before calorific foods, such as gravy-laden beef casseroles.

Camera shy Have you noticed the dearth of cat photographs on the internet? This is due to cats being painfully camera shy.

Canine If the attraction of dogs is really only about fetching sticks, cats have got that covered, so what's all the fuss about?

Om...

CANINE

CAREFREE

Carefree One of the most carefree of animals, nothing worries the domestic cat – except of course the sight of dwindling food supplies.

Careful Don't scold Kitty when she jumps up to grab that plate balanced precariously at the edge of the table. She's just making sure it doesn't fall.

CAREFUL

Caring No matter what your problem is, or how long it takes to tell someone about it, you can always rely on your cat to care.

CARING

Carpet cleaner Your cat is absolutely vigilant about keeping your rare and expensive Persian carpet steam-cleaned – which is why he throws up on it so regularly. He's only making sure your high standards don't slip.

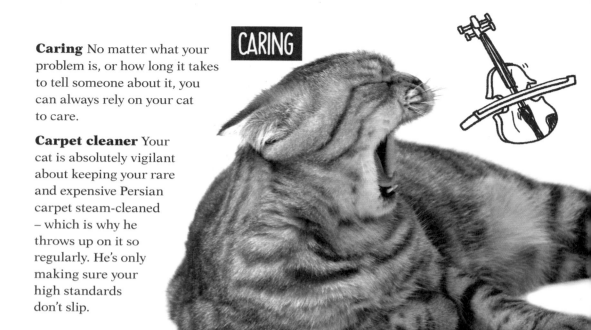

CARPET CLEANER

CEREBRAL

Cerebral Cats are always on the lookout for a brain-stimulating exercise, such as madly clawing their way out of a cardboard box or running at breakneck speed up and down the hallway in pursuit of imaginary foes.

CHARACTER ACTOR

Character actor You may have seen cats in costumes. These are not hard-done-by pets who have been unwillingly dressed up by their owners, but professional character actors. Favourite roles include pirates, royalty and pumpkins.

CLINGY

Clingy Cats can be clingy, sticking to you like glue, never wanting to be apart for a moment.

COMPETITIVE

Competitive If you're pitted against a cat in a game of skill or dexterity, just give up now. The fiercely competitive nature of domestic cats makes them impossible to beat. However, cats have been known to 'take a fall' in exchange for extra portions of tuna jerky.

Compliant The good thing about cats is their malleable nature and willingness to join in the fun, such as going for a Sunday stroll with the family. Who needs a dog!

Congenial Always friendly and considerate creatures, even while sitting in a box a cat will always try to select one with a peephole so they can continue to shoot the breeze with you.

COMPLIANT

CONGENIAL

Conscientious When you give a cat a job – whether it's scratching the carpet to lift the pile, or napping on the sheets in the cupboard to warm them up – they will always do it, and do it well.

Conservationist If you see your cat climbing onto the birdfeeder, don't panic. It's more than likely that your cat is simply carrying out research into birdlife. Cats are passionate about the plight and future of birds – for purely unselfish reasons of course.

CONSIDERATE

Considerate Cats are always looking for ways in which to help you further, such as stretching out on the best seat in the house, just to selflessly keep it warm for you.

Cooperative During flea-ing time or when it's time to visit the vet, you can be confident that your cat will always cooperate.

Couture Whether it's a scarf artlessly wrapped around the body, or a fleecy blanket attached to a claw and dragged behind, cats just have that 'je ne sais quoi' when it comes to fashion.

COOPERATIVE

COUTURE

26

CREATIVE

Creative Just give a cat a ball of wool or a tube of paint and a paintbrush and then leave them alone for a few hours. You will be stunned by the results.

Critical Your cat will often leave constructive 'reviews' of the latest brand of cut-price cat food that you bought in bulk. You'll mostly find these reviews on the hall carpet or in other helpfully obvious places around the house.

Cryptic Sometimes, even with the best will in the world, it's just impossible to understand what your cat is saying to you.

CRITICAL

CRYPTIC

is for...

DATA ENTRY

DECISIVE

Data entry Where there's a keyboard, there's usually a cat to be found tirelessly entering important data. Of course it would be far more helpful if they remembered to switch the computer on first – and if they typed in any of the 6500 known human languages.

Decisive Once a cat makes a decision, such as whether to go outside or not, that's that.

Decorator Although somewhat iconoclastic in their approach to home decorating, just give a cat five minutes with a piece of flimsy, expensive fabric, and they will artfully customise it for you.

DECORATOR

DEFERENTIAL

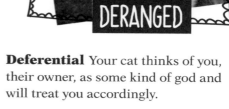

DERANGED

DELICATE

Deferential Your cat thinks of you, their owner, as some kind of god and will treat you accordingly.

Delicate When it comes to those jobs that require a gentle touch, like dressing the Christmas tree with super-fragile glass baubles, your cat is the ideal helper.

Deranged The plethora of clown-based horror movies and TV shows has taken its toll on cats too.

Devoted No matter whether you fall out over portion control or repeatedly forget to change your cat's litter, you can be safe in the knowledge that your cat will remain totally devoted.

Dignified Cats are admired for their grace and their human owners always treat them with due respect.

Dog-friendly It might look like this cat has the puppy in a headlock, but he is just exhibiting extreme joy at the return of the lovable pooch from next door who loves to share Kitty's food.

DEVOTED

DIGNIFIED

DOG-FRIENDLY

is for...

Eager When Kitty sees you getting the guitar out for your daily practice session, she knows she's in for a real treat.

Eagle-eyed A cat's field of vision is 200 degrees – as opposed to the human's mere 180, and they can even see in the dark. So there's no way any small rodents are going to be able to sneak past this baby!

Early adopter
As soon as a new tech device enters the home, the cats will be the first to master it – especially any new apps for home delivery from the pet food store or live streaming of Garfield cartoon re-runs.

EAGER

EAGLE-EYED

EARLY ADOPTER

Easy care The best thing about cats is that they require almost no upkeep. They are fastidiously clean and never leave a mess.

Eavesdropper Be careful when discussing sensitive issues near cats as they are terrible eavesdroppers. They might seem to be in a fugue state while grooming, but you can be sure they are storing away all that juicy info.

Empathetic Have you noticed when you're feeling sad or lonely your cat will come up to you and look concerned and anxious? It's absolutely heart-warming – until you notice that it's just that their bowl is empty.

Engaged Cats can listen to you for hours on end. However, it does help if there's a bug sitting on the wall behind your head.

Enthusiastic Some people say that dogs are more fun because of their constant enthusiasm. But cats can be virtual fireballs of excitement when roused.

Epicurean It's nothing but the very best for cats. If you're not giving them 'Three Paw' chef standard food or higher, they'll go and find it themselves.

EVIL GENIUS

Evil genius Just look into his eyes. That's the visage of an evil genius, plotting world domination.

Executive Cats are born business leaders. Have you noticed their propensity for hanging around office equipment and sleeping on staplers? Next time your cat suggests investing in shrimp farming, you should maybe listen.

EXECUTIVE

EXISTENTIAL

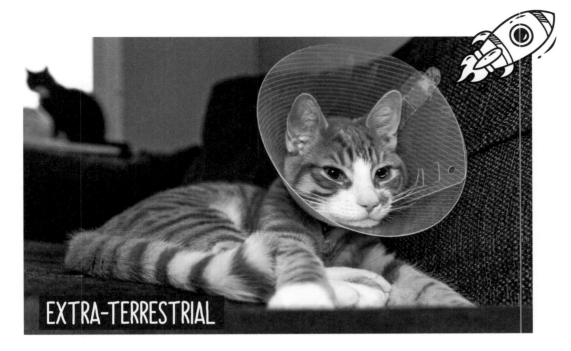

EXTRA-TERRESTRIAL

Existential Cats tend to avoid mirrors as they can result in an existential crisis.

Extra-terrestrial They walk among us. Those plastic satellite dishes round cats' necks? Don't be fooled that they're there for 'medical reasons'.

Extroverted Cats enjoy a good party. However, they may have to seek safety in a drawer to avoid their paws being trampled by catnip-infused humans doing the Funky Chicken.

EXTROVERTED

is for . . .

Familiar In days of old cats had a bad name, mainly due to identity theft by supernatural beings, or 'familiars', who consorted with witches and other unsavoury characters.

Fantasist No matter how many thousands of times your cat attempts to catch that little red bug and fails, he knows that one day it's going to be 'Hasta la vista, Baby' for that pesky critter.

Fashion victim Someone should ask those cats often seen posing in jaunty hats and gawdy scarves if they got dressed in the dark. We're not buying the excuse that their owner dressed them up without their permission.

FAMILIAR

FASHION VICTIM

FANTASIST

Ferocious It's no wonder that some people are terrified of cats. I mean, just look at her! A sabre-toothed tiger in miniature.

Fertiliser Cats like to contribute however they can in order to make your home and garden a more beautiful and fragrant place. Those tulips needed a little extra assistance.

Festive As soon as the holiday decorations make an appearance, your cat makes a dash for his costume rack to grab the reindeer antlers. It's quite a job wrestling them off him once the festive season is over.

FEROCIOUS

FESTIVE

FERTILISER

Fetishistic Have you noticed how a cat likes to jump on and sift through your clothes if you leave a freshly washed pile unattended? They're checking the labels to see if there's anything in their size.

Fire guard One of the most gruelling of chores for the domestic cat is that of official fire guard. However, someone needs to remind the cat that the idea is to guard it, not hog it.

FETISHISTIC

FIRE GUARD

FIXER UPPER

Fixer upper Those cats congregating around dumped sofas are just calculating the possible profits of fixing them up and selling them on.

Flight simulator Cats are drawn to boxes that remind them of planes. They're not usually lucky enough to score a window seat when travelling.

Fluffy Cats have about 60,000 hairs per sqare inch on their back, and 120,000 per square inch on their undersides.

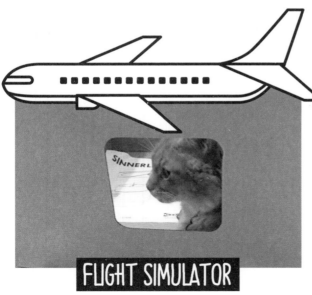

FLIGHT SIMULATOR

FLUFFY

Folk dancing Cats love traditional folk dancing. As soon as they've managed to press-gang the required number of couples, before you can say do-si-do, they've rolled away with a half sashay.

FOLK DANCING

Forgiving Sure, you might have worked late and forgotten to buy your cat some food. But she doesn't mind at all filling up on those out-of-date stale cat biscuits that she refused to eat the first time – when they were fresh.

Fragrant The great thing about cats is how clean they are. They never give off a smell of sweaty socks or wet wool, but rather are redolent of a fresh summer breeze.

FORGIVING

FRAGRANT

French polisher There's no need to go to the inordinate expense of hiring professional French polishers to touch up your costly antiques when your cat is champing at the bit to give it a go.

Frenetic The energy of the household cat is legendary. It's amazing how much ground they can cover in the two hours they're awake each day.

Frugal Cats have a strong sense of the future and never guzzle their food all in one go, preferring to keep most of it stored away for a rainy day.

FRUGAL

FRENETIC

FUEL-INJECTED

Fuel-injected When they hear their human owner's keys jingling to open the front door, cats can actually create a vacuum as they run full pelt down the hallway to greet them.

Funambulist The art of funambulism, or tightrope walking, was invented by a cat. His only access to the street was by walking along a narrow fence, flanked on one side by a garden inhabited by a rottweiler and on the other a garden with a doberman.

FUNAMBULIST

is for...

GAME KEEPER

Game keeper If you happen to keep game birds or chickens, you couldn't do better than to ask your cat to keep an eye on them for you. He'll be more than willing.

Gangsta Gangsta is a subgenre of the urban street cat cult. The gang members often adopt a threatening expression as well as aggressively loud collars and accessories.

GANGSTA

Generous Cats have a charitable nature and will always give you all the time you need when you initiate a lengthy stop-and-pat session with them.

GENEROUS

Gossipy Some cats spend half their day hanging over the next door cat's fence gossiping. Is Twinkle at Number 15 pregnant or is she just stacking on weight?

Gothic Years of watching Gothic movies and TV shows has confused many household cats, who now believe they possess magical powers.

Grateful Cats are always overjoyed and immensely grateful for any big-ticket item you buy for them. In fact, the bigger the better, as they just can't wait to get their paws on the box it came in.

GOSSIPY

GOTHIC

GRATEFUL

GREEN-PAWED

GREGARIOUS

GUILELESS

Green-pawed If you have a houseplant that's on its last legs, just give your cat half an hour with it. He knows what he's doing.

Gregarious Cats are friendly and fearless and never make a run for the nearest bolt-hole when cat-obsessed female relatives pop in for a cup of tea.

Guileless The domestic cat is a complete stranger to the word 'manipulation'. She has positively no notion of how rolling around and looking winsome might just get her that fourth breakfast.

is for . . .

HAIR ARTISTE

HANDY

HAPPY-GO-LUCKY

Hair artiste Don't bother taking Fido to the poodle parlour. Your cat is available anytime to give him a short back and sides.

Handy Cats are ready and willing to muck in and help with those DIY jobs around the house – but mainly when ladders are involved.

Happy-go-lucky Cats are of a sanguine disposition and never mind if they are unceremoniously put outside when your friend with the cat allergy is visiting.

HARMONIST

La la la la

HARDWORKING

Hardworking If you see your cat asleep on piles of paperwork in the office, that's probably because he's been burning the midnight oil trying to get things in order for you.

Harmonist Cats are great singers and will practise that one particular note over and over and over until they get it just right.

Healthy Luckily cats never need to diet as they are naturally drawn to low-calorie foods. They will never eat rubbish, even if they are literally surrounded by temptation.

HEALTHY

Fresh Delicious

HEINOUS

HELPFUL

Heinous There are some cats that are just so wicked and badly behaved that there's no point reprimanding them. Just embrace their wild spirit.

Helpful Your cat is obsessive about the cleanliness of your keyboard. She can always be found cleaning it with her own built-in feather duster.

Homeopathic Like many humans, cats are interested in alternative therapies and natural remedies. Catnip is for purely medicinal purposes and is definitely not a recreational drug, even though it might appear otherwise to the untrained human eye.

HOMEOPATHIC

HUMANE

HOSPITABLE

Hospitable Sharing and caring by nature, you will find your cat is very receptive to allowing newcomers into her personal chillout area – eventually.

Humane Sure, cats are natural predators, but you can take comfort in the knowledge that they are always humane and would never go in for anything awful like torturing their victim first.

Hydropathic Cats adore water and when things pile up and get too much for them, a dose of hydrotherapy is just what the vet ordered.

HYDROPATHIC

Hygienic Don't worry about whether your cat may have licked that freshly baked pie when you left him alone in the room with it for five minutes. Cats always sanitise their tongues after a vigorous cleaning of all their nooks and crannies.

Hyperactive Where do cats get all that energy from? It's go go go as soon as they get up at the crack of noon right up until sleeptime at 1 pm.

Hypochondriac Cats are terrible worriers when it comes to their health. They're always examining themselves and browsing through medical encyclopaedias. That next vet checkup can't come soon enough!

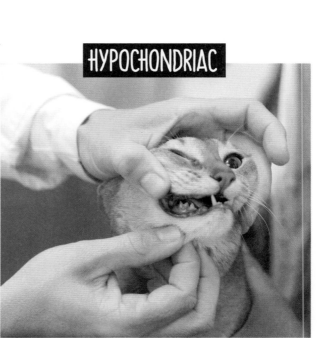

HYGIENIC

HYPOCHONDRIAC

HYPERACTIVE

L is for...

ICHTHYOLOGIST

Ichthyologist After many years of tough tertiary training in order to become ichthyologists, or 'fish scientists', cats can often be seen carrying out piscatorial behavioural studies near fish ponds or goldfish bowls.

Imaginative The phrase 'make it work' was surely invented by and for cats.

Impassioned Cats bring enthusiasm and passion to everything they do, whether it's making themselves into a living obstacle course in a busy thoroughfare, or sulking about the new 'healthy' brand of cat food, which comes in noticeably smaller-sized tins.

IMAGINATIVE

IMPASSIONED

INCONSPICUOUS

INFLUENCER

INNOCENT

Innocent If you come home to find your favourite mug smashed on the floor and Kitty lying beside it, don't be so quick to judge. His story about an intruding three-legged dog might well be true.

Inoffensive You never need to worry when you have important visitors. Cats always know how to behave appropriately.

Inquisitive Cats are curious. In fact, it's more accurate to say they are pathologically nosy. They can often be seen twitching the curtains and peeking through blinds in order to see what the neighbour's cat is up to.

Inconspicuous Cats are natural hunters and their variously coloured coats allow them to blend into the background when in pursuit of their prey.

Influencer We all know that cats have controlled the internet for years, specifically targeting the cat-obsessed segment of the market to purchase larger and larger tins of cat food in bigger and bigger quantities.

INQUISITIVE

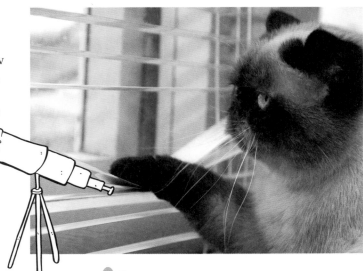

59

Insomniac It's amazing to think how cats cope, as they are often stricken by crippling insomnia. They may only be surviving on 15 hours of sleep per day.

Interested Your cat hangs on your every word. There's nothing he enjoys more when you come home from work than listening to a blow-by-blow description of your extraordinary meeting on how to reduce paper-clip wastage.

Interpretive dancer Not content with vocalisations to express their jubilance or dismay, cats turn to the art of interpretive dance to ensure you well and truly get the message.

INSOMNIAC

INTERESTED

INTERPRETIVE DANCER

INTIMIDATING

Intimidating Cats have a way of finding the weak spot in dogs and ruthlessly using it against them until the dog is completely in their power.

Intrepid While the thrill of shinnying up drain pipes to the roof, or climbing to the highest branches of trees is natural for cats, the question of getting down again might not be. It might become necessary to yowl for human staff armed with ladders, or request that an urgent call is put through to the local fire department.

Invisible Cats know that if they can't see you, you obviously can't see them.

INTREPID

INVISIBLE

is for...

JACUZZI-LOVER

JAILBREAKER

JAZZ PAWS

Jacuzzi-lover Lovers of luxury and pampering, cats enjoy nothing better than jumping into the sink at the end of a busy day – it's just a matter of waiting until a human kindly comes along to turn the tap on.

Jailbreaker Those cats in wire cages aren't on their way to the vet. Their portable prisons are the last resort for the ultimate escape artists – the Steve McQueens of the feline world.

Jazz paws Every time the strains of a Bob Fosse Broadway musical number are heard on the radio, it's jazz paws all the way and your cat will treat you to an improvised tap solo or soft paw shuffle.

JEDI

JET-PROPELLED

Jedi Like all Jedi masters, the cat values knowledge and wisdom above all things – except sausages.

Jet-propelled Rather like a jump jet, able to take off vertically, a cat is capable of a similar motion when faced with the terrifying sight of a cucumber that has rolled out of the crisper drawer of the refrigerator.

Jobless Cats aren't lazy. They are always looking for work – preferably as a cage cleaner at the local bird sanctuary.

JOBLESS

JOCULAR

Jocular You'll often see cats stop to pass the time of day with friends. The sound of their laughter can be heard for miles.

Judgemental When getting dressed for a hot date, it can be disconcerting when your cat's face is clearly saying to you, 'Are you planning to leave the house dressed like that?'.

Justified If you're going to make cookies in the shape of a cat, your cat will be fully justified in assuming they have been created for her delectation.

JUDGEMENTAL

JUSTIFIED

is for ...

KID-FRIENDLY

'KIT' BOXER

Kid-friendly There's nothing your cat loves more than a visit from Little Johnny down the road, who is keen on hours of enthusiastic hugs and squeezes.

'Kit' boxer Cats are masters of many martial arts, including their own variation of kick boxing known as 'kit' boxing. This self-defence method is mainly for use against persistent dogs.

Kitchen hand When you go into the kitchen and your cat hurriedly follows you in, he's not expecting an early dinner. He's only there to see if there's anything he can help you with. Just think of him as your own personal sous chef. If a sausage happens to fall to the floor he'll be straight onto it.

KITCHEN HAND

is for . . .

LACTOSE-INTOLERANT

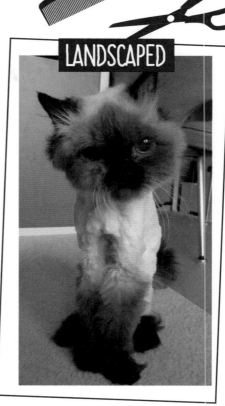

LANDSCAPED

Lactose-intolerant Cats are allergic to lactose and that's why you'll never ever find them anywhere near ice cream, milk, cream or any other dairy products that happen to be lying around looking delicious.

Landscaped Unfortunately drastic landscaping, or 'catscaping', is necessary during the hottest months. If cats are not happy with the results, they will go into voluntary exile until they are fit to rejoin society.

Lateral thinker Cats just think better when they're lying down. It's as simple as that.

LATERAL THINKER

LAW-ABIDING

Law-abiding You can always leave your cat alone with fresh fish, safe in the knowledge that she would never attempt a heist.

Lawnmower There's no need to get someone in to mow the lawn. Cats love eating grass and can do it for you – as long as you don't mind the eight weeks it will take them to finish the job.

Life guard Cats can often be seen hanging around fish bowls and aquariums, tirelessly watching over the inhabitants, ready to give mouth-to-mouth resuscitation if required.

LAWNMOWER

LIFE GUARD

Logical When your cat exhibits unusual behaviours, such as climbing into a garden umbrella and becoming hopelessly tangled in its workings, there's obviously a logical reason for this. Don't question him.

Loving Cats are affectionate by nature and love to snuggle up to you for hours, purring and nuzzling and melting your heart. But only if the radiator isn't on.

Loyal Cats are totally monogamous. There is no way that the vicious rumour could be true that your cat belongs to four different families in the street as well as the fish and chip shop on the corner.

is for...

MALNOURISHED

Malnourished As far as your cat's concerned, if her bowl isn't overflowing, starvation is imminent.

Market researcher You will often see your cat door-knocking in your street. He's usually carrying out personal market research into what the general consensus is on cat food portion size.

Martyr When you 'ground' Kitty for leaving the remains of a small rodent on your pillow, she will punish you by sulking for a full seven minutes.

MARKET RESEARCHER

MARTYR

MASSEUR

Masseur Cats can be seen constantly kneading and massaging everything in sight, from your favourite cashmere jumper to the family dog. They are just in training for their professional massage diploma.

Master of disguise On some occasions, such as worming or flea-ing day, your cat will prove impossible to find. This is probably because they have donned one of their many perplexing disguises.

Mellifluous Some skills can't be taught, they are just innate, such as the remarkable vocal range of the Siamese cat.

MASTER OF DISGUISE

MELLIFLUOUS

Motor mechanic
Cats are car obsessed and can often be found lying under the family saloon for hours, just tinkering away making various improvements.

Musical Many cats are proficient at the piano. Being four-footed gives them an advantage as they can play a piece designed for two pairs of hands on their own.

Mystical Cats have various supernatural powers, the most notable being mind control. Cats will often sit staring at you – for hours if necessary – until they have bent you to their will and made you forget that you've already fed them dinner three times that day.

MUSICAL

MYSTICAL

MOTOR MECHANIC

75

is for...

NAME-CALLER

NARRATOR

NAUTICAL

Name-caller Have you ever wondered what your cat is saying to you after you've informed her for the tenth time that there will be no seconds? It's probably best you never find out.

Narrator When your favourite television show is on, your cat will position himself on top of or in front of the screen, narrating and helpfully pointing out things you might otherwise have missed.

Nautical For centuries, cats have sailed the high seas and kitty commodores run a tight ship. When it's anchors aweigh, it's all paws on deck for a three-hour nap.

77

Neighbourly Cats are among the most neighbourly of domestic animals and will often physically display to visiting cats just how glad they are to see them.

News hound Have you ever asked why your cat insists on sitting on the newspaper so you can't get to it? He simply wants to check the news first to ensure there is nothing that might upset you.

Ninja When walking under trees, watch out! The Tree Ninja Cat may be hiding and won't hesitate to carry out a surprise attack – especially if you are on your way home from the fishmonger.

NEIGHBOURLY

NEWS HOUND

NINJA

NOBLE

NOT-FOR-PROFIT

Noble There can be no doubt that cats are of noble birth and are the ruling class. Just take a look at the space on your bed that is allotted to the cat, and you'll soon realise who's in charge.

Not-for-profit Cats require very little in order to be happy – other than the weekly pallet-load of cat food tins, a pantry overflowing with treats of every description and permanent access to the best seat in the house in front of the fire.

is for . . .

OBEDIENT

OCCUPATIONAL THERAPIST

ONLINE DATER

Obedient Your cat would like to live by the letter of your law, but it's the semi-final at Catfight Club tonight.

Occupational therapist If you work from home, your cat will always position herself close by to observe your posture and general work practices.

Online dater When you are on the laptop, your cat can often be found lurking nearby. He's waiting for you to take a bathroom break so he can check his online dating profile.

OPPORTUNISTIC

ORATOR

ORGANISED

Opportunistic Every leaky tap is an opportunity. Cats will do everything they can to prevent the plumber from reaching the house in order to fix it.

Orator Be wary of buying your cat a platform. If you do, brace yourself for hours of rhetorical speechmaking on the subject of cats' rights.

Organised When there's a suitcase to be packed, your cat will always be there, offering unsolicited organisational advice.

OVER ACHIEVER

Ornamental If you aren't able to afford your own ornaments to adorn your shelves, maybe your cat could stand in until you can.

Outgoing Cats are known for their uninhibited and predictable nature and can always be relied on to be the life and soul of the party.

Over achiever After that record-breaking two-hour bed bath, it's no wonder your cat is exhausted.

is for...

PALAEONTOLOGIST

Palaeontologist When you see your cat digging up your newly planted vegetable plot, don't get angry. It's probably just another palaeontological dig in search of sabre-toothed tiger remains.

Palm reader Your cat can tell a lot about you by putting his paw in your palm – mainly whether you are holding any treats.

PALM READER

Parapsychologist If there was ever any doubt that ghosts and spirits exist, just observe your cat. Can she see a ghostly veiled figure in the corner of the room that is not of this world, or is it just another cockroach?

PARAPSYCHOLOGIST

PATIENT

PEDANTIC

PENITENT

Patient Most cats understand that you are very busy and are happy for you to take your time in preparing their dinner.

Pedantic If you utter the words 'you've had enough', the over-pedantic cat will spend the evening flicking through texts and googling, looking for references to support his proposition about the correct food to cat weight ratio.

Penitent It might just look like your cat is sleeping with her paws over her eyes to avoid the light, but in fact she's in anguish with guilt for all the litter she's trailed through the house, and for the unfortunate 'accident' on the new rug.

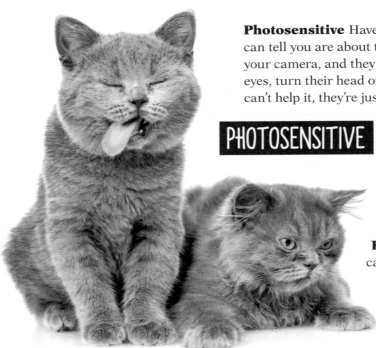

Photosensitive Have you noticed how your cats can tell you are about to press the shutter button on your camera, and they will immediately close their eyes, turn their head or make a stupid face? They can't help it, they're just photosensitive.

PHOTOSENSITIVE

Picky Cats are extremely fussy eaters and some human owners' feelings can be hurt when they see their cat foraging in the garbage bin after rejecting their homemade cat food.

Plausible If you spring your cat rummaging around in the refrigerator, maybe his story about hearing a cry for help from inside could possibly be true?

PICKY

PLAUSIBLE

PLAYFUL

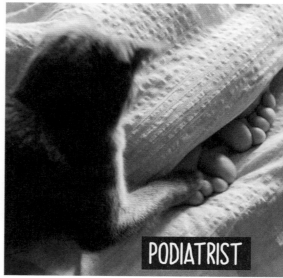

PODIATRIST

POLE DANCER

Playful There's nothing a cat enjoys more than quality playtime with their human owner – as long as it's on their terms and to their schedule.

Podiatrist If you are in bed and feel your cat scratching at your exposed feet, she's just carrying out a podiatric examination free of charge, checking for ingrown toenails and assessing whether it's time for you to get the compression stockings out.

Pole dancer It's a little known fact that the art of pole dancing was inspired by the way cats interact with their scratching posts. When you consider pole dancing moves, such as the 'Birman Bumslide' and the 'Devon Rex Dip', it all becomes blindingly obvious.

POP LOCKIN

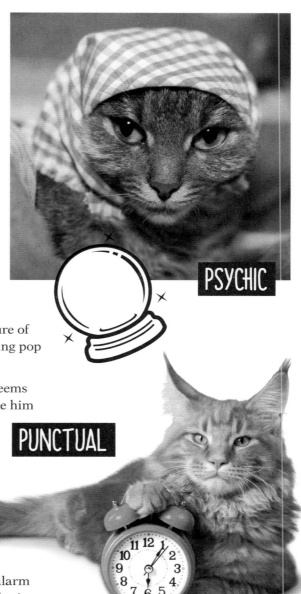

PSYCHIC

Pop lockin The flexible bone structure of the domestic cat makes for some styling pop and lock and robot dancing skills.

Psychic It's uncanny how your cat seems to know when you're just about to take him to the cattery, and finds the hiding place of the century at the padlocked building site down the street.

PUNCTUAL

Punctual The domestic cat is such a stickler for good time-keeping that they will wake you at dawn, fearing your alarm clock might malfunction and you will miss their breakfast time.

is for . . .

Qualified When you complain to your cat about chewing the fairy lights and she tells you she's a qualified electrician, you should believe her. What do you think she's been doing during those hours when she disappears each day? She's been studying for her certificate in electro-engineering.

QUALIFIED

Quantity surveyor The job of quantity surveying is somewhat different in the feline world.

Quick-witted Cats are remarkably intelligent, apart from the fact that they believe that feather on a stick is a real bird.

QUANTITY SURVEYOR

QUICK-WITTED

is for . . .

RAMPANT

REALIST

RECEPTIONIST

Rampant The traditional image of the rampant lion, famously seen on medieval coats of arms, is based on the familiar 'begging for treats' pose, which is common to all the cat family.

Realist The cat is fully aware of his strengths and limitations, except when it comes to the size of his stomach.

Receptionist Cats have excellent front-of-house skills, which is why you will often be greeted at your destination by a Concierge Cat.

RECRUITER

REMOTE-HOGGER

RESTROOM MONITOR

Recruiter You'll often see cats attempting to recruit young pups before they are experienced enough to buy into that whole 'Dogs vs Cats' thing.

Remote-hogger Your cat is happy to watch TV with you, but only if they are allowed to keep control of the remotes.

Restroom monitor One of the domestic cat's favourite jobs is that of restroom monitor. It's their job to accompany humans to the bathroom and keep an eye on proceedings. They are extremely put out if a human attempts to 'go it alone' without their assistance.

Retro When it comes to entertainment centres, cats prefer the good old, vintage record player. It's far more comfortable than a smartphone.

Roofer One of the oldest professions known to domestic cats is that of roofing. It's in their blood. Even if they aren't professional roofers, they just can't help themselves. They're up on the roof on a daily basis, checking the apron flashing and caulking.

Rubber-necker If there's a 'scene' going on in the street outside, your cat just won't remove herself from the window. In fact she'll insist on your opening the window so she can hear the kerfuffle more clearly.

RETRO

RUBBER-NECKER

ROOFER

is for...

SATISFIED

Satisfied It's hard to begrudge a cat pestering you for food, as it's always such a pleasure seeing their satisfied expression when you place their dinner bowl in front of them.

Scientific Don't be fooled by a cat with his head wrapped in toilet paper. He is not wilfully destroying your supplies. He is far more likely to be carrying out important, controlled experiments in quantum physics, examining the nature of toilet paper at a subatomic level.

SCIENTIFIC

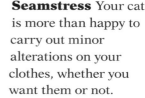

SEAMSTRESS

Seamstress Your cat is more than happy to carry out minor alterations on your clothes, whether you want them or not.

SECURITY SHREDDER

SHAPE SHIFTER

SHOE TESTER

Security shredder If you're lax about your personal security, your cat's got your back. She will immediately shred any paperwork that is left lying around – sensitive or otherwise.

Shape shifter It's been suggested that cats are not altogether a solid. They are capable of transforming themselves into whatever shape they desire, be it the shape of your most fragile vase or that of your designer boots.

Shoe tester Cats are duty-bound to carry out endurance and sniff tests on all human shoes.

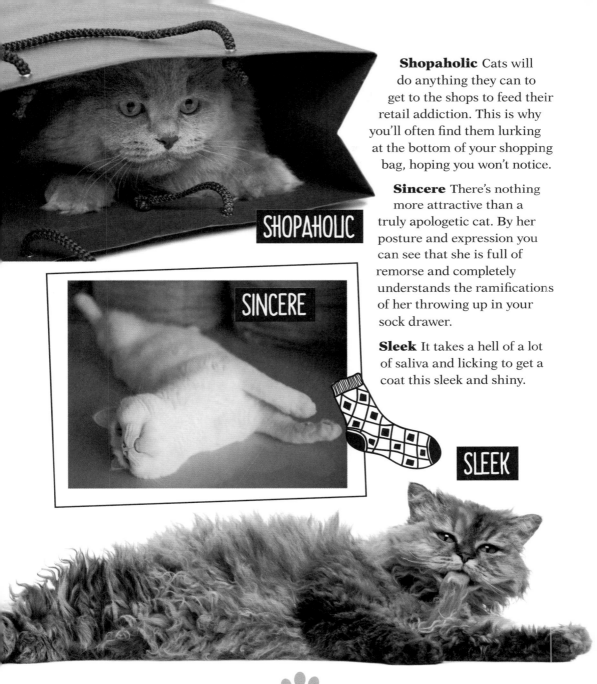

Shopaholic Cats will do anything they can to get to the shops to feed their retail addiction. This is why you'll often find them lurking at the bottom of your shopping bag, hoping you won't notice.

SHOPAHOLIC

Sincere There's nothing more attractive than a truly apologetic cat. By her posture and expression you can see that she is full of remorse and completely understands the ramifications of her throwing up in your sock drawer.

SINCERE

Sleek It takes a hell of a lot of saliva and licking to get a coat this sleek and shiny.

SLEEK

SOCIAL CLIMBER

SOLAR-POWERED

Social climber Cosying up to Fifi the pampered Persian at Number 56 could be important to your cat, as he might get access to her split-level marble litterbox and jungle gym.

Solar-powered It's vital for cats to spend at least two hours in the sun each day in order to power up enough to achieve the required energy for napping.

SONIC BOOM

Sonic boom The sound of a cat breaking the sound barrier and causing a sonic boom can often be heard seconds after opening a refrigerator door.

SPACE CADET

SPATIALLY AWARE

Space cadet Cats have been in astronaut training programs for over 50 years – they're not going to hang around once earth's sardine supply runs out.

Spatially aware Cats can calculate the comfort of a bowl or box to the nearest picolitre.

Spy Cats are masters of espionage. However, they rarely bring back any intelligence as they are usually asleep within seconds of reaching their observation post.

SPY

STATUESQUE

STUNTCAT

Statuesque The body builders of the feline world, Sphynx cats choose to 'shave down' in order to better show off their remarkable physiques.

Stoic Every day the average house cat stoically withstands hours of patting and being addressed by names such as 'Mr Fluff Fluff Pants' and 'Baby Boo Boo'.

Stuntcat Many young cats are attracted to the glamour of becoming a movie stuntcat. You will often see them practising around the house attempting death-defying leaps and falls.

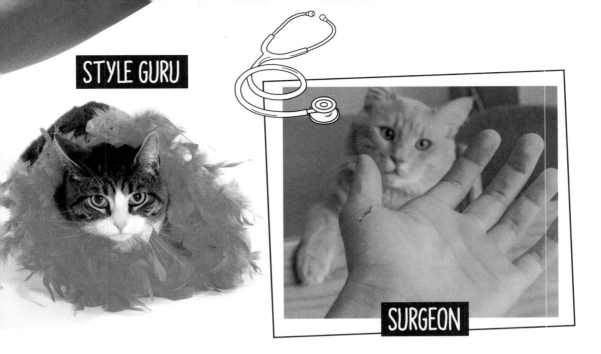

STYLE GURU

SURGEON

SVELTE

Style guru There are some stylish cats who call the shots as far as feline fashion goes. If they say pink feather boas are in, they're in and your cat won't stop pestering you until they get one.

Surgeon Fascinated by human anatomy, cats sometimes get the urge to make a small incision and just have a bit of a look.

Svelte It's not easy to look this good. But a tough daily regime of 20 leg lifts seems to do the trick.

is for...

Tasteful The cat, like its majestic big cat cousins roaming the savanna, is a beautiful creature of remarkable grace.

TASTEFUL

Team player It can be an advantage for your cat to stay on good terms with the household dog, as you never know when it will be necessary to buddy up with Rover in order to stage a SWAT team-style siege on the fridge at midnight.

TEAM PLAYER

Tech savvy If there's something wrong with your laptop, just call the IT Kitties. They'll be there in a flash to help – just remember to switch off the aquarium screensaver first if you want to get any sense out of them.

TECH SAVVY

TEETOTAL

TELEKINETIC

THEATRICAL

Teetotal For centuries cats have been teetotal and therefore immune from the dangers of alcohol. However, the recent introduction of catnip wine has the potential to change everything.

Telekinetic If you see your cat staring hard at a stationary object, they are more than likely honing their telekinetic skills. These could come in handy if you're not around at feeding time.

Theatrical Oh, the fuss a cat can make if you buy pilchards instead of sardines.

TOLERANT

TOP-DRAWER

TOUCHY FEELY

Tolerant It's just so cute when Benjy the Husky lies on top of Giles the cat for 'big hugs'. It's obvious that Giles loves it!

Top-drawer Being a superior species, it's nothing but the top drawer for cats – especially when it contains clothes made of luxury fabrics, which are great for getting one's claws into.

Touchy feely Most cats adore being patted for hours on end by their human owners. However, there are some unscrupulous felines who are prepared to fake it as they are just 'in it for the chicken'.

TRAINABLE

TRANSPORTABLE

TREE SURGEON

Trainable Just like dogs, cats can also be trained to play ball games and fetch, but it may take several years to get your cat to the first stage, which is to look at the ball.

Transportable Cats adore car travel but they prefer a window seat so they can feel the wind in their fur.

Tree surgeon What is it that your cat is doing up that tree? Is she helpfully thinning the crown, or does she have more sinister motives?

Trend slave Is your cat one of those who slavishly follows fashions, no matter how ridiculous they might be? Remember that fad for dressing up as a bird and sitting in a nest in a tree? At least I think it was just a fashion trend...

Trustworthy Cats mix well with other animals. They are particularly fond of small rodents, such as hamsters and guinea pigs. You can tell how much your cat enjoys their company by the inordinate amount of time he spends watching over his tiny furry friends, especially when they are frolicking on the lawn in their open-topped cage.

TREND SLAVE

TRUSTWORTHY

is for...

Uncomfortable If there are no old boxes to hand, your poor cat will be forced to seek refuge in one of the many expensive luxury cat beds you have bought them over the years.

Uncomplaining It's always the same story with my cat. Why oh why can't I just leave the fridge door open so he can help himself and what's wrong with fifteen meals a day?

Underfed If you are even a minute late in preparing your cat's dinner, they will sit by and heckle you mercilessly until the food hits their bowl.

UNDERFED

UNYIELDING

UNSPOILT

Unspoilt Despite the padded, velvet cat-sized chair, the five duck-down cat beds and the Tiffany's diamond-encrusted food bowl, Jemima remains remarkably unspoilt.

Unyielding When a cat has set his mind on something, there is nothing you can do to change it – except perhaps tickle his tummy.

Upbeat They may look slothful, but in their minds these cats are in hot pursuit of a gang of fieldmice.

UPBEAT

Upholsterer Unless you invest in a cat-proof couch, you will be treated to random reupholstering on a regular basis.

Useful Cats are great to have around for all those unusual jobs that never get done. Those flowers aren't going to smell themselves!

UPHOLSTERER

User-friendly Unfortunately cats don't come with an instruction manual so you'll just have to work out Kitty's likes and dislikes through trial and error.

USER-FRIENDLY

USEFUL

is for...

VEGETARIAN

Vegetarian People who have put their cats on vegetarian diets swear they much prefer it.

Viceless Cats would never take a bribe in exchange for a cuddle.

Virtuous When your cat greets you in the morning full of smiles and affection, it's possible that there may have been a furball incident during the night.

VICELESS

VIRTUOUS

is for . . .

Waitstaff Your cat likes to jump up onto the dining table to check everything is to your satisfaction.

Weapon of mass destruction Meet Frank, the 'Feline Fixer'.

Weather watcher On rainy days your cat will be glued to the window, looking for a break in the clouds. They must be at their post outside when the kids come past after school bearing treats.

WAITSTAFF

WEATHER WATCHER

WEAPON OF MASS DESTRUCTION

Weight-conscious
When weighing your cat, first check that she hasn't 'fiddled' with the dial.

Welcoming For many people the idea of their cat eagerly watching for them to get home and then rushing up to nuzzle them is but a pipe dream.

Well mannered Apart from cleaning their private parts during dinner and hacking up furballs in your bedroom, cats are models of decorum.

WELCOMING

WEIGHT-CONSCIOUS

WELL MANNERED

WILLING

WIND INSTRUMENT

WOOKIE

Willing You can put a leash on a cat and take him for a walk, but you can't make him enjoy it.

Wind instrument If you don't think you've ever experienced cat flatulence before, believe me, you'd know if you had.

Wookie In the 1970s the 'Chewbacca Look' became popular for cats, particularly Persians. You still see some old-timers around valiantly keeping the style going.

X is for...

XENODOCHIAL

XERIC

XYLOTOMOUS

Xenodochial Cats are xenodochial, or friendly to strangers, by nature and are more than happy to welcome new cats into the household, but it's less of a bloodbath if both cats are on opposing sides of a door.

Xeric Cats generally prefer a xeric, or dry, environment. However, after discovering the joy of a dripping tap, some cats will recklessly attempt to progress to Stage 2 – the bubble bath.

Xylotomous When your cat scratches on your bedroom door in the middle of the night, she can't help it. As with woodpeckers and all other xylotomous, or wood-boring, creatures it's instinct.

is for...

YOGA MASTER

YARDARM

YOLO

Yardarm If you're not lucky enough to own a yardarm, you can have a drink when the sun passes over the cat instead.

Yoga master Cats are undoubtedly wonderful at yoga, but they only know three positions – downward cat, hungry cat and sleeping cat.

YOLO Although having been warned to keep away from the washing machine on numerous occasions, one day Ralph saw the door was open and thought, 'What's the worst that could happen?'.

is for . . .

ZEALOUS

ZESTFUL

Zealous When the vacuum cleaner comes out, some cats run for cover, while other cats, who are zealous about their appearance, take the opportunity to have a full fur fluff-up.

Zestful Your high-energy kitten might look as though she's finally gone to sleep, but she's probably just resting her eyes while dreaming up exactly what her next act of household carnage will be.

ZOMBIFIED

Zombified 'Zombified' is really just another word for 'hungry'. You may have noticed that zombies are always after food, rather like the domestic cat, whose expression can be uncannily similar to that of a zombie at times.

PHOTOGRAPHIC CREDITS

iStockphoto: back cover (bottom) 10 (top left), 13 (bottom right), 15 (bottom left and right), 16 (bottom right), 17 (top right), 19 (top right), 20 (bottom right), 21 (top and bottom), 22 (bottom), 23 (top left), 24 (bottom right), 29 (bottom), 30 (top left and bottom), 31 (top), 33 (centre), 35 (top right), 39 (bottom left and right), 40 (bottom left), 42 (top and bottom right), 43 (top and centre), 45 (top), 49 (bottom), 51 (top right), 55 (bottom left and right), 60 (bottom), 63 (top left and right), 64 (top right and bottom), 65, 67 (top right), 69 (bottom), 70, 73 (top), 74 (bottom right), 77 (top left and right), 85 (top and centre),
86 (centre), 87 (bottom left), 93 (bottom), 97 (top), 98 (top left), 99 (bottom), 100, 103 (top right and bottom), 105 (top), 106 (top left), 107 (bottom), 109 (top), 111 (top left), 112 (top left), 115 (top), 117 (top), 118 (top), 119 (bottom), 123 (top left and bottom), 125 (centre).

Joy Cornish: 78 (bottom right), 108 (bottom).

Shutterstock: front cover, back cover (top), all letter opener illustrations, 6, 8, 9 (top), 10 (top right and bottom), 11, 12, 13 (top and bottom left), 16 (bottom left), 17 (top left and bottom), 20 (top and bottom left), 21 (centre), 22 (top), 23 (top right and bottom), 24 (bottom left), 25, 26, 27, 29 (top left and right), 30 (centre), 31 (bottom left and right), 33 (top), 34, 35 (top left and bottom), 36 (top left), 37, 39 (top), 40 (top and bottom right), 41 (bottom), 43 (bottom), 44, 45 (bottom), 47, 48 (top and bottom right), 49 (top left and right), 51 (top left and bottom), 52 (top left and right), 53, 54, 55 (top), 57, 58, 59, 60 (top), 61, 67 (top left and bottom), 69 (top left), 71, 73 (centre and bottom), 74 (top and bottom left), 75 (top and bottom left), 77 (bottom), 78 (top and bottom left), 79, 81, 82 (top left and right), 83 (top right and bottom), 85 (bottom), 86 (top and bottom), 87 (top and bottom right), 88, 89, 91, 93 (top left and right), 94, 95 (bottom left and right), 97 (centre and bottom), 98 (top right and bottom), 99 (top and centre), 101 (top right and bottom), 102, 103 (top left), 105 (centre and bottom), 106 (top right and bottom), 107 (top and centre), 108 (top left and right), 109 (bottom), 111 (top left and right), 112 (top right), 113, 115 (bottom left and right), 117 (bottom left and right), 118 (bottom left and right), 119 (top left and right), 121, 123 (top right), 125 (top and bottom).

Pete Smith: 9 (bottom), 19 (top left), 36 (bottom left), 42 (bottom left), 48 (bottom left), 52 (bottom), 60 (centre), 63 (top right), 64 (top left), 83 (top left), 127.

Yasmine Wick Kopita: 15 (top), 16 (top), 19 (bottom), 24 (top), 33 (bottom), 33 (bottom), 36 (bottom right), 41 (top), 69 (top right), 75 (bottom right), 82 (bottom), 95 (top), 101 (top left), 112 (bottom).

ACKNOWLEDGEMENTS

Ariana and Pete would like to thank Paul McNally of Smith Street Books for once again championing the cause of cats getting the attention they so desperately need. Thanks to the incredibly talented Emilia Toia for her fantastic design concept. Special thanks to the amazing Kerry Klinner for going above and beyond the call of duty in bringing the whole book design together in record time, and to Pam Dunne for running her eagle eye over the text.

Thanks to our friends who supplied photos of their beloved cats: Yasmine Wick Kopita, Maxwell Kopita and Jay Kopita for photos of Babs, BooBoo Kitty, Dexter and Kimba; and Joy Cornish for photos of Mookie and Lily.

Loving thanks to Lou, Brenda, Mal, Neville, Beverley, Amanda, Michael, Tim, Serge and Serena.

And last, but certainly not least, thanks to our ginger fluffball and 'muse', Alfie. Without him this book would not have been possible.

Published in 2017 by Smith Street Books
Melbourne • Australia
smithstreetbooks.com

In association with Ariana Klepac Publishing
Sydney • Australia

ISBN 978-192541834-7

CIP data is available from the National Library of Australia

Design concept: Emilia Toia
Layout: Kerry Klinner, Megacity Design

Printed and bound in China by C&C Offset Printing Co. Ltd.

Book 31
10 9 8 7 6 5 4 3 2 1